ᑯᕕᓲᑦ
KUVISUUT
THINGS THAT POUR

ᐅᓇ ᐃᒻᒧᒃ.

Una immuk.

This is milk.

ᐅᓇ ᐃᒥᖅ.

Una imiq.

This is water.

ᐅᓇ ᐃᒥᒐᒃᓴᖅ.

Una imigaksaq.

This is juice.

ᐅᓇ ᑏ.

Una tii.

This is tea.

ᐅᖅᓱᕈᑎᒃᓴᖅ.

Una uqsurutiksaq.

This is cooking oil.

Nunavummi

Nunavummi Reading Series

The Nunavummi reading series is a Nunavut-developed levelled book series that supports literacy development while teaching readers about the people, traditions, and environment of the Canadian Arctic.

Level 3

- 8–12 pages
- One word per page
- No punctuation
- Highly supportive images help readers decode the words

4

- 8–12 pages
- One sentence per page
- Sentences are very short, basic, and repetitive
- Basic punctuation (periods only)
- Highly supportive images help readers decode the sentences

Level 5

- 8–12 pages
- One sentence per page
- Sentences become longer and more varied
- Punctuation includes mostly periods, with very few question marks and exclamation marks
- Highly supportive images help readers decode the sentences

Fountas & Pinnell Text Level: A

This book has been officially levelled using the F&P Text Level Gradient™ Leveling System.

ᐅᖃᓕᒫᒐᖅ ᓴᖅᑭᔮᖅᑎᑦᑎᓂᐊᖅᑐᖅ
ᑯᕕᓲᓂᒃ, ᓲᕐᓗ ᐃᒥᖅ ᐊᒻᒪ ᐃᒥᒐᒃᓴᖅ.

Uqalimaagaq saqqijaaqtittiniaqtuq
kuvisuunik, suurlu imiq amma imigaksaq.

This book features things that pour,
such as water and juice.

LEVEL 4

Nunavummi

Fountas & Pinnell
Text Level: A

ISBN 978-1-77450-008-8

9 781774 500088